JOHN RUTTER

# PSALMFEST

FOR SOPRANO AND TENOR SOLI,
MIXED CHOIR, AND ORCHESTRA

MUSIC DEPARTMENT

OXFORD
UNIVERSITY PRESS

*Oxford University Press, Walton Street, Oxford OX2 6DP, England*
*Oxford University Press Inc., 198 Madison Avenue, New York, NY 10016, USA*

*Oxford is a trade mark of Oxford University Press*

*© Oxford University Press 1996*

*All rights reserved. Apart from any fair dealing for the purposes of research or private study, or criticism or review, as permitted under the Copyright, Designs and Patents Act, 1988, this publication may only be reproduced, stored or transmitted, in any form or by any means, with the prior permission in writing of Oxford University Press.*

*Permission to perform the work in public (except in the course of divine worship) should normally be obtained from the Performing Right Society Ltd. (PRS), 29/33 Berners Street, London W1P 4AA, or its affiliated Societies in each country throughout the world, unless the owner or occupier of the premises being used holds a licence from the Society.*

*Permission to make a recording must be obtained in advance from the Mechanical Copyright Protection Society Ltd. (MCPS), Elgar House, 41 Streatham High Road, London, SW16 1ER, or its affiliated Societies in each country throughout the world.*

*Music typeset on Sibelius 7*

# CONTENTS



The first performance of *Psalmfest* was given on 8 June 1993 in the Morton Meyerson Symphony Center, Dallas, by the combined high school choirs of Garland, Texas, conducted by the composer. The same choirs and conductor repeated the work on 13 June 1993 in Carnegie Hall, New York.

*Composer's note:*

The nine movements of *Psalmfest* were written over a period of some twenty years. Seven of them have been published separately as anthems; *Cantate Domino*, written in 1991, has not hitherto appeared in print, and *O how amiable are thy dwellings* was composed specially for *Psalmfest*. In gathering these psalm settings together, my aim was to open them up for concert as well as liturgical use. To the same end, I have added soprano and tenor soloists and orchestrated those movements which existed only with organ or ensemble accompaniments.

The complete work lasts 45 minutes, and conductors should feel free to shorten it by omitting one or more movements. In particular they may prefer to leave out *The Lord is my shepherd*, which has previously appeared in my choral work *Requiem*. If soloists are not available, *O how amiable are thy dwellings* may be omitted and the solo portions of movements 2, 4, and 6 sung chorally.

Conductors need to decide whether or not the soloists should sing in *I will lift up mine eyes*. The soprano soloist's part is rather low-lying, and if this proves uncomfortable for the singer, it might be better to perform the whole movement in its original, purely choral form.

No. 9 being for double choir, it is advisable for the chorus to be placed in antiphonal layout throughout the work (which will enable the 'half choir' passages in no. 5 to be sung antiphonally). If the work is perfomed without no. 9 (perhaps with no. 7 as a finale), the chorus can be placed in normal single choir layout, in which case the 'half choir' passages in no. 5 should be sung by full choir or by a semi-chorus.

# INSTRUMENTATION

*Psalmfest* is available in two different instrumentations (both intended for players of professional standard):

**1. for full orchestra:**

2 flutes (2nd doubling piccolo)
2 oboes
2 clarinets
2 bassoons
4 horns in F
3 trumpets in B flat and C
3 trombones (2 tenor, 1 bass)
tuba
3 pedal timpani
percussion*
harp
strings

*2 players: glockenspiel, xylophone, suspended cymbal, crash cymbals, snare drum, tambourine

The instrumentation of each movement is as follows:

Nos. 1, 3, and 9: full orchestra
No. 2: 2fl, 2ob, 2cl, 2bsn, 2hn, timp, hp, str
No. 4: ob, hp, str
No. 5: choir unaccompanied
No. 6: cl, hp, str
No. 7: 2fl (2nd doubling picc), 2ob, 2cl, 2bsn, 2hn, 2tpt, timp, perc, hp, str
No. 8: 2fl, hp, str

**2. for chamber ensemble with organ:**

flute
oboe
clarinet in B flat
3 pedal timpani (optional)
percussion* (optional)
harp
organ

*2 players: as for orchestral version

All performing material for both versions is available on hire from the publisher.

For texts see p. 90

Duration: 45 minutes

# PSALMFEST

JOHN RUTTER

## 1. O be joyful in the Lord

Psalm 100

This movement is also available separately, with organ accompaniment (Oxford Anthems A346).


© Oxford University Press 1984 (this movement)
© Oxford University Press 1996 (complete work)



Printed in Great Britain

OXFORD UNIVERSITY PRESS, MUSIC DEPARTMENT, GREAT CLARENDON STREET, OXFORD OX2 6DP



Photocopying this copyright material is ILLEGAL.

16
A
unis.
serve the Lord with glad - ness,
lands:
serve the Lord with
unis.
A
22
unis.
(♪ = ♪)
and come be - fore his pre - sence with a song.
glad - ness,
(♪ = ♪)
28
B
ALTOS f
SOPRANOS f
Be ye sure, be ye sure that the Lord he is
be ye sure he is
TENORS
BASSES
f Be ye sure that the Lord he is God:
B

36
our -
God: it is he that hath made us, and not we our -
Ped.
42
- selves;
C
SOPRANOS mf più legato
- selves, and not we our - selves; we are his peo - ple, and the sheep of his
TENORS
mf più legato
dim.
mf
Ped.
49
D
ALTOS f marcato
pas - ture. O go your way in - to his gates with
BASSES
f marcato
legato
f
Ped.

56
SOPRANOS f marcato
thanks - giv - ing,
O go your way in - to his gates with
TENORS
f marcato
non legato
63
S. f
E
A.
with thanks - giv - ing,
T.
B. f
70
cresc.
F
ff
and in - to his courts with praise:

G Dolce e tranquillo ( ♩ = ♩. of preceding )
ALTOS mp legato
Be thank-ful un-to him, and speak
mf legato
dim.
mp legato
SOPRANOS
mp
(SOPS.)
good of his Name. Be thank-ful un-to him, and speak good of his Name.
Be thank-ful un-to him, and speak good of his
TENORS
mp
H
ALTOS mp
S.
mf
his mer-cy is ev-er-last-ing: and his
A.
Name.
T.
p cresc.
For the Lord is gra-cious,
BASSES
B. mf
dim.
p cresc.
mp
cresc.

106
cresc.
f
dim.
I Tempo I ( ♩. = 66 )
p
truth en - dur - eth from ge - ne - ra - tion to ge - ne - ra - tion.
cresc.
en - dur - eth
dim.
p
I Tempo I ( ♩. = 66 )
mf cresc.
f
dim.
p legato
Ped.
115
TENORS
O be joy - ful in the Lord, all ye lands, O be joy - ful in the
BASSES
p cresc.
mp cresc.
cresc.
mp cresc.
Ped.
123
ALTOS mf cresc.
SOPRANOS
f
cresc.
Lord, all ye lands, O be joy - ful in the Lord, all ye lands, O be joy - ful
mf cresc.
f
cresc.
mf cresc.
f
cresc.

130
J
ff
in the Lord, all ye lands.
Glo - ry
ff
J non legato
ff
138
be to the Fa - ther;
glo - ry be to the Son:
dim.
and to the
dim.
146
mf
unis.
(mf) cresc.
K
f
As it was in the be - gin - ning,
Ho - ly Ghost;
is
As it was in the be - gin - ning,
unis.
mf cresc.
mf
cresc.

153
L
f
now, and ev-er shall be:
is now, and ev-er shall be:
world with - out end,
world with - out
legato
Ped.
161
cresc.
Largamente
rit.
ff
world with - out end.
A - men, a
end, world with - out end.
A
169
M a tempo
(senza rall.)
-men.
-men.
8va
fff

# 2. I will lift up mine eyes

Psalm 121

Note: The seven-beat bars in this movement fall into groups of 2 + 2 + 3 beats except where indicated otherwise by brackets.
* See preface.
Also available separately, with organ accompaniment (A313).

© Oxford University Press 1976, 1996

23
SOPRANOS
p dolce e legato
ALTOS
I will lift up mine eyes unto the
TENORS
BASSES
p dolce e legato
27
unis. mp
hills: from whence come-eth my help. My help
unis. mp
mp espress.
31
B
cresc.
mf
f
com - eth e-ven from the Lord: who hath made hea - ven and
cresc.
mf
f
B
cresc.
mf
f

35
mf
C
earth.
BASSES (or TENOR SOLO)
mp
He will not suf - fer thy foot to be moved:
mf
mp
39
TENORS (or TENOR SOLO)
mp
mf
and he that keep-eth thee will not sleep.
43
D
ALTOS (or SOPRANO SOLO)
mp dolce
Be-hold, he that keep - eth Is - ra - el shall nei - ther
p
Ped.
47
slum - ber nor sleep, shall nei - ther slum - ber

E
(ALTOS)
nor sleep.
mp cantabile
(con Ped. sempre)
cresc.
F TENORS and BASSES (or TENOR SOLO)
unis. mp dolce cantabile
The Lord himself is thy keeper: the Lord is thy defence upon thy right hand;
SOPRANOS and ALTOS unis. (or SOPRANO SOLO)
So that the sun shall not burn thee by day:
(unis.)

71
mp
unis.
nei - ther the moon by night.
mp
G
75
pp molto espress. e calmo
(FULL CHOIR)
The Lord shall pre - serve thee from all e - vil:
pp molto espress. e calmo
G
pp
p
mp cantabile espress.
79
yea, it is e - ven
he that shall keep thy soul.
he that shall keep
he that shall keep
pp
p espress.

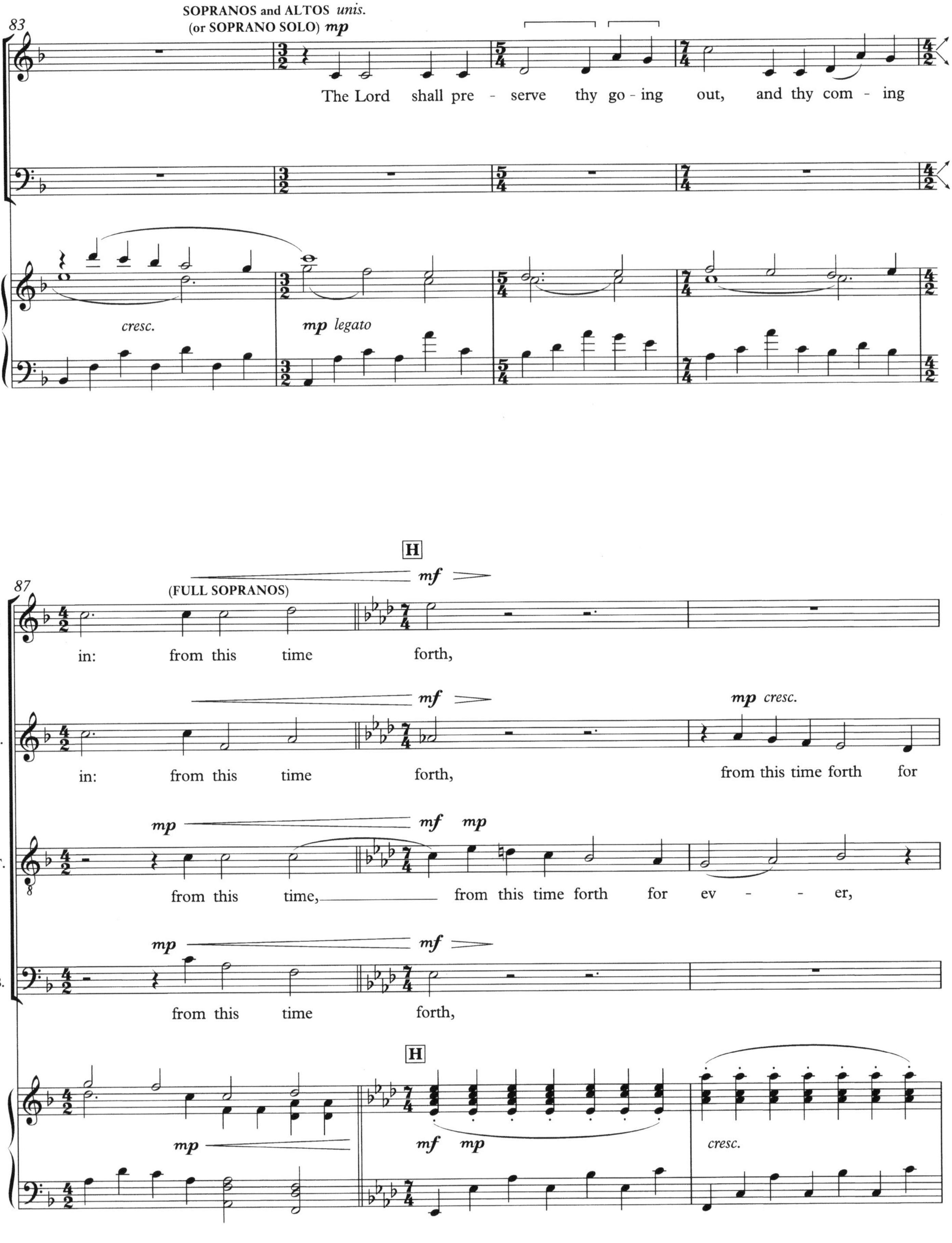

87

H

S. (FULL SOPRANOS) mf
in: from this time forth,

A. mf mp cresc.
in: from this time forth, from this time forth for

T. mp mf mp
from this time, from this time forth for ev - - er,

B. mp mf
from this time forth,

H

mp
mf mp
cresc.

90
poco accel.
from this time forth for ev - er,
from this time forth for
ev - er,
from this time forth for ev - er,
from this time forth,
from this time forth,
from this time
mf
mf cresc.
f
cresc.
93
(non accel.)
poco rit.
a tempo – molto tranquillo al fine
ev - er,
from this time forth for ev - er,
from this time forth for ev - er and for ev - er,
forth, from this time forth for ev - er,
ff
I

97
SOPRANOS mf dolce dim.
for ev - er,
ALTOS mp dim.
for
TENORS for ev - er,
mf dolce
BASSES for ev - er,
mp
dim.
mp
101
(ALTOS)
p dim.
pp
ev - er and ev - er - more.
TENORS for ev - er - more.
BASSES p dim.
pp
dim.
p
dim.
pp
Ped.
J SOPRANOS and ALTOS
105
pp
A - men, a - men.
pp
J
Ped.

109
p
S.
A - men, a - - - - men.
A.
A - men, a - - - - men.
T.
A - men, a - - - - men.
B.
A - men, a - - - - men.
p
7
Ped.
113
mf
ten.
rit.
p dim.
pp
A - - - - - - - - men.
A - - - - - - - - men.
A - - - - - - - - men.
A - - - - - - men.
rit.
ten.
mf
p dim.
pp
Ped.

# 3. Praise the Lord, O my soul

Psalm 146

* Sopranos or altos may divide, at conductor's discretion.

Also available separately, with accompaniment for organ, or for organ with timpani and brass ensemble (A330).

© Oxford University Press 1981, 1996

A
(♪ = ♪)
mf
prai - ses un - to my God.
O put not your trust in prin - ces, nor in
mf
O put not your
A
(♪ = ♪)
mf
dim.
p
B
p legato
a - ny child of man:
for there is no help in them.
For when the
trust in man:
dim.
p
B
p legato
dim.
mp
(♩ = ♩)
cresc.
mp
pp
breath of man go - eth forth he shall turn a - gain to his earth: and then all his thoughts
cresc.
mp
pp
(♩ = ♩)
mp
pp

30
C
SOPRANOS
mf brightly
pe - rish.
Bless - ed is he that hath the
TENORS
mf brightly
C
mp cresc.
mf
34
f legato
God of Ja - cob for his help:
and whose hope is in the Lord his
f legato
39
S.
f marcato
A.
God;
Who made heav'n and earth, the sea, and all that there - in
T.
B.
f marcato
marcato cresc.
f
Ped.

45
cresc.
ff
is: who keep - eth his pro - mise for ev - er;
cresc.
ff
Ped.
51
SOPRANOS
D
mf legato espress.
Who help-eth them to right that suf-fer wrong: who feed - eth the hun-gry.
TENORS and BASSES
The
mp legato dolce
D
mf dolce
mp
57
mf
f
Lord loos-eth men out of pri - son:
the Lord giv - eth sight to the
mf
f
mf
f

62
dim.
mp
E
blind.
The Lord help-eth
dim.
mp
mp legato espress.
E
dim.
mf
mp
Ped.
67
mp legato espress.
p dolce e legato
the Lord car-eth for the right-eous.
The
them that are fall - en:
p dolce e legato
72
Lord car-eth for the stran-gers; he de - fend - eth the fa-ther-less and wi - dow:
p
mp
3

77
mf
as for the way of the un - god - ly, he turn-eth it up - side down. The
mf
f
cresc.
Ped.
F Poco largamente
82
Si - on,
Lord thy God, O Si - on, shall be King for ev - er - more: and through -
Si - on,
dim.
3/2
4/4
mf
Ped.
87
ritard.
mp
a tempo ( ♩ = 144 )
- out all ge - ne - ra - tions.
p
mp cresc.
mf cresc.
f

92
G
f marcato
Glo - ry be — to — the Fa - ther, glo - ry be — to the
f marcato
G
3
f marcato
96
Fa - ther, and — to the Son, and to — the Ho - ly Ghost; As it was in the be -
was, —
mf
100
H
mf
- gin - ning, is now, and ev - er shall be: world with - out end. — A - men, —
— is now,
mf
3
mf
H
3

104
f
world with - out end. A - men,
world with - out end. A - men,
cresc.
f
cresc.
f
108
ff
a - men.
ff
ff
112
(senza rit.)
(senza rit.)
fff
sffz

# 4. The Lord is my shepherd

Psalm 23

The original version of this movement (for mixed choir and organ) is available separately (385629 8).

© Oxford University Press Inc. 1978, 1996

28
B
forth be - side the wa - ters of com - fort.
TENOR SOLO
mp
He shall con - vert my
B
mp
34
soul:
and bring me forth in the paths of right - eous - ness,
3
mf
(SOPRANO SOLO)
40
mp
for his Name's sake,
p
for his Name's sake.
mp dim.
for his Name's sake,
p
for his Name's sake.
mp
dim.
p

46
C
S.
A.
T.
B.
CHOIR
Yea, though I walk thro' the val - ley of the sha - dow of death, I will fear no
53
e - vil: For thou art with me; thy rod_ and thy staff com - fort me.
59
D
Thou shalt pre - pare a ta - ble for me a - gainst them that

65
mp
trou - ble me:
thou hast a - noint - ed my head with
mp
mp
p
69
rit.
E a tempo
oil, and my cup shall be full.
rit.
E a tempo
mf
poco a poco dim.
pp
Ped.
76
SOPRANO SOLO
p tranquillo
But thy lov - ing kind - ness and mer - cy
TENOR SOLO
p tranquillo
But thy lov - ing kind - ness and mer - cy
p
Ped.

82
S.
mp cresc.
F
f
shall fol-low me all the days of my life:
A.
CHOIR
And I will dwell in the house
T.
shall fol-low me all the days of my life:
B.
mp cresc.
f
F
cresc.
mp
f
88
dim.
mf
dim.
mp
dim.
of the Lord,
in the
house
of the
Lord
house,
in the
house
of the
dim.
mf
dim.
mp
dim.
house
of the
Lord
dim.
mf dim.
mp
dim.
94
for
ev - er,
p
dim.
pp
rit.
Lord
for
ev - - er,
for
ev - - - - - - er.
p
dim.
pp
rit.
p
dim.
pp

# 5. Cantate Domino

*(choir unaccompanied)*

from Psalm 96

*for rehearsal only

© Oxford University Press 1996

19
A
mf
p
f
ff
dim.
- te, can - ta - te. O sing un-to the Lord a new song:
- cum, can - ta - te. O sing un-to the Lord a new song:
30
cresc.
sing un-to the Lord, all the whole earth. Sing un-to the Lord, and praise his

B
(♪ = ♪)
ff mf cresc. f mp
Name: be tell-ing of his sal - va-tion from day to day.
Name: be tell-ing of his sal - va-tion from day to day.
ff mf cresc. f (f)
Name: be tell-ing of his sal - va-tion from day to day. Can - ta - te Do - mi - no can - ti-cum
Name: be tell-ing of his sal - va-tion from day to day. Can - ta - te Do - mi - no can - ti-cum
C
mf p f
Can - ta - te Do - mi - no can - ti-cum no-vum, can - ti - cum no - vum. De-
Can - ta - te Do - mi - no can - ti-cum no-vum, can - ti - cum no - vum. De-
mf p f mf
no-vum, can - ta - te Do - mi - no can - ti-cum no-vum, can - ti - cum no - vum. De-clare
no - vum, can - ti - cum no - vum. De-clare

60
p
-clare his ho - nour un-to the hea-then: and his won - ders, his won - ders un-to
his ho - nour un - to them: and his won - ders, his won - ders un-to
69
D
mf
f
all peo-ple. For the Lord is great, for the Lord is
cresc.

77
ff
f
great,
and can - not wor - thi - ly be praised:
mf più legato
he is more to be
86
feared than all gods.
mp
he is more to be feared than all gods,
he is more to be feared than all gods.
dim.
pp

*If the choir is seated antiphonally (see preface), Choir 1 should sing this section.

112
G
(♪ = ♪ sempre)
-vens, the Lord that made the hea - vens.
-vens, the Lord that made the hea - vens.
-vens, the Lord that made the hea - vens. Glo-ry and wor-ship are be - fore him:
the Lord that made the hea - vens. Glo-ry and wor-ship are be - fore him:
122
H
pow-er and ho-nour are in his sanc-tua - ry. A - scribe un-to the Lord the
pow-er and ho-nour are in his sanc-tua - ry. A - scribe un-to the Lord the
pow-er and ho-nour are in his sanc-tua - ry. A - scribe un-to the Lord the
pow-er and ho-nour are in his sanc-tua - ry. A - scribe un-to the Lord the

*If the choir is seated antiphonally, Choir 2 should sing this section.

151
FULL CHOIR
p
mf
f
whole earth stand in awe of him. Let the heav'ns re - joice, and let the earth be glad: for he
J
157
cresc.
mp cresc.
mf solenne
mp
com - eth, he com - eth, he com - eth, he com - eth, he com - eth to

*Melody and words of *Veni Creator Spiritus* 9th century

186
L
Tempo I - Vivace (♩. = 66)
pp
mp
pec-to-ra.
Can-ta-te Do-mi-no can-ti-cum
p brightly
pec-to-ra. Can-ta-te Do-mi-no can-ti-cum no-vum:
195
(♪ = ♪)
stringendo
mf
cresc.
f
ff
no-vum, can-ta-te Do-mi-no, can-ta-te Do-mi-no, can-ta-te, can-ta-te, can-ta-te,
no-vum, can-ta-te, can-ta-te Do-mi-no, can-ta-te, can-ta-te, can-ta-te,
can-ti-cum no-vum, no-vum, can-ta-te, can-ta-te, can-ta-te,

M
A tempo giusto, con gioia
204
(ff)
can - ta - te Do - mi - no can - ti - cum no - vum, can - ta - te Do - mi - no can - ti - cum
can - - - - - ta - - - te, can - ta - te Do - mi - no can - ti - cum
can - - - - - ta - - - te, can - ti - cum no - -
211
mf subito
f
allargando
a tempo vivace
S. 1 no - - - - vum,
div.
cresc.
ff
no - vum, can - ti - cum no - vum, can - ti - cum, S.2 can - ti - cum no - vum.
no - vum, can - ti - cum no - vum, can - ti - cum, can - ti - cum no - vum.
- vum, no - - - vum, can - ti - cum, can - ti - cum no - vum.

# 6. The Lord is my light and my salvation

from Psalm 27

Also available separately, with accompaniment for clarinet and organ (A379). In the USA, available from Hinshaw Music, Inc. (HMC-1064).

© Oxford University Press 1989, 1996

17
poco accel.
whom then shall I be a-fraid, of whom then shall I be a-fraid?
poco accel.
mf
B Poco più mosso (♩ = 76)
20
mp
mf
S.
A.
Though an host of men were laid a-gainst me, yet shall not my heart be a-fraid: and though there rose up
T.
B.
mp
mf
B Poco più mosso (♩ = 76)
mp
mf
mp
Ped.
24
f
poco rall.
mf dim.
Tempo I (♩ = 66–69)
mp
war a-gainst me, yet will I put my trust in him.
f
mf dim.
mp
poco rall.
Tempo I (♩ = 66–69)
f
mf dim.
mp
Ped.
Ped.

C
SOPRANO SOLO
p dolce
One thing have I de-sired of the Lord, which I will re-quire:
p dolce
e-ven that I may dwell in the house of the Lord all the days of my life, to be-hold the fair beau-ty of the
mp
mp
D
poco accel.
Tempo II ( ♩ = 76 )
Lord, and to vi-sit his tem-ple.
p
mp
mf
E
BASSES
mp
For in the time of trou-ble he shall
mp
p

55
TENORS and BASSES
mp
hide me in his tab - er - na - cle: yea, in the se - cret place of his dwell - ing shall he
60
F
SOPRANOS and ALTOS unis.
f risoluto
and set me
hide me, and set me up up - on a — rock of stone,
unis.
mf
f risoluto
F
mf
f
64
up up - on a rock of stone.
unis.
maestoso
mf

68
G Brightly ( ♪ = ♪ of preceding = 152 )
SOPRANOS and ALTOS
unis.
mf poco leggiero
There-fore will I
TENORS and BASSES
unis.
There-fore will I of - fer in his dwell - ing an ob - la - tion,
mf poco leggiero
p
G Brightly ( ♪ = ♪ of preceding = 152 )
mp
mf
Ped.
74
of - fer in his dwell - ing an ob - la - tion with
great glad-ness, with great glad-ness, with great
an ob - la - tion with
f
mf
f
80
ff
H
f
glad - ness:
I will sing, and speak
I will sing, and speak prai - ses un - to the Lord,
unis.
ff
f
H
ff
f
mf leggiero
Ped.
Ped.

85
prai - ses un - to the Lord,
sing, and speak prai - ses
I will sing, and speak prai - ses,
f
cresc.
89
ff
(Tempo II ♩ = 76)
un - to the Lord.
ff
(Tempo II ♩ = 76)
ff
f poco marc.
mf
J
94
p legato
cresc.
mp
Heark-en un - to my voice, O Lord, when I cry un - to thee: have mer - cy up - on me, and
p legato
p cresc.
mp
J
p legato
mp

99
mp
p
hear me. My heart hath talked of thee, Seek ye my face: Thy face, Lord, will I seek.
O
p
mp
K
105
ALTOS
mp
nor cast thy ser - vant a -
(+ TENORS)
hide not thou thy face from me, hide not thou thy face from me:
cresc.
mf
cresc.
mf
mp
L
111
poco rall.
SOPRANO SOLO
Tempo I (♩ = 66–69)
p dolce
- way in dis - plea - sure.
Thou hast been my suc - cour:
p
dolce

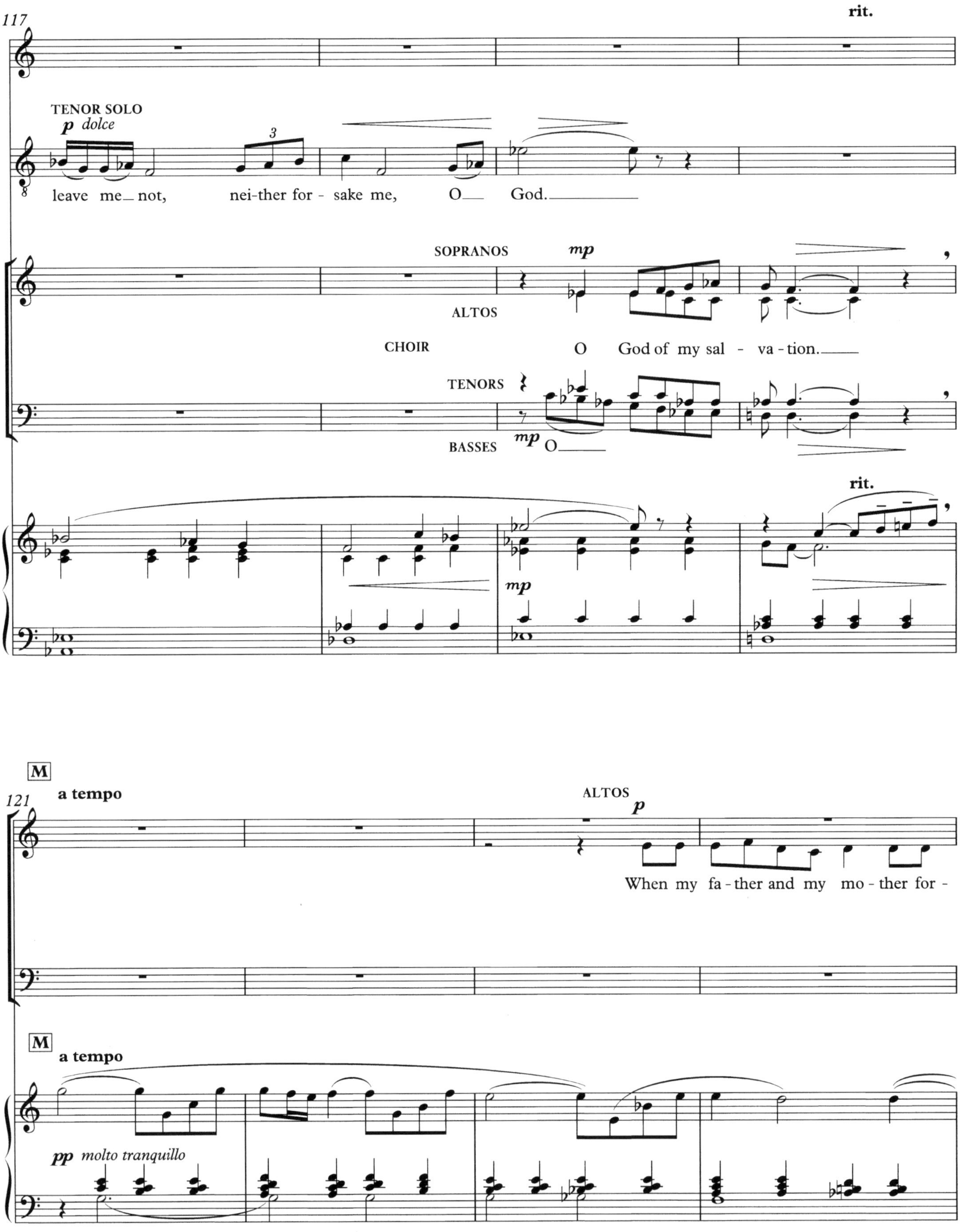

117

**rit.**

TENOR SOLO

*p dolce*

leave me — not, nei-ther for - sake me, O — God. —

SOPRANOS *mp*

ALTOS

CHOIR

O God of my sal - va - tion. —

TENORS

BASSES *mp* O —

**rit.**

125
( + SOPRANOS )
p
cresc.
mp cresc.
mf cresc.
- sake — me: — the Lord ta - keth me up, ta - keth me up, the Lord ta - keth me
mp cresc.
mf cresc.
p cresc.
mp cresc.
mf cresc.
Ped.
129
poco f
N
mf dolce
up. be strong, and he shall
Be strong,
poco f
mf dolce
N
poco f
mf dolce
Ped.
132
mf
com - fort thine heart, be strong, be
he shall com - fort thine heart;
mp
mf
mp
mf
Ped.

135
mp
dim.
pp
strong, and he shall com - fort thine heart, he shall com - fort thine heart; and
mp
dim.
pp
mp
dim.
p
pp
138
put thou thy trust in the Lord.
141
pp
rit.
ppp
Put thy trust in the Lord, in the Lord.
pp
ppp
rit.
ppp

# 7. O clap your hands

Psalm 47, vv. 1–7

Also available separately, with organ accompaniment (A307).

© Oxford University Press 1973, 1996

13
sing un-to God with the voice of me - lo - dy.
4
A
( ♪ = ♪ )
18
For the Lord is high, and to be feared:
f
Ped.
24
cresc.
ff
f
he is the great King up - on all the
legato

B
29
ALTOS mp tranquillo
He shall sub -
earth.
B
non legato
dim.
legato
mp tranquillo
34
SOPRANOS
and ALTOS
unis. mp
-due the peo - ple un - der us:
and the na - tions
un-der our
39
SOPRANOS mp legato
feet.
He shall choose out an he-ri-tage for us:
TENORS
mp legato
legato sempre

44
ALTOS
mf legato
e - ven the wor - ship of Ja - cob, whom he
BASSES
mf legato
cresc.
mf
48
SOPRANOS
C
f marc.
ALTOS
loved.
God is gone up with a mer - ry noise,
TENORS
BASSES
f marc.
C
f
52
with a mer - ry noise,
with a mer - ry noise:
f
non legato
Ped.
*
Ped.
*

56
(f)
(♪ = ♪)
and the Lord with the sound of the
allargando
D Largamente (♩ = c.116)
60
ff
trump.
O sing prai - ses, sing
marc.
cresc.
65
prai - ses un - to our God:
O sing prai - ses, sing prai - ses un - to our
3

(ff) molto maestoso
King. For God is the King of all the earth: sing ye
praises with un - der - stand - ing.
prai - ses
dim.
mp accelerando
E
p cresc.
Tempo I (♩ = 132)
f
O clap your hands to - ge - ther, all ye peo - ple:
f marc.
Ped.

83
mp cresc.
O clap your hands, clap your hands,
mf
dim.
mp
cresc.
Ped.
87
mf cresc.
clap your hands, clap your hands, clap your hands to - ge - ther, all ye peo - ple,
f
sim.
91
cresc.
ff
allargando
clap your hands to - ge - ther, all ye peo - ple, clap your hands, all ye
3

F
a tempo
(non dim.)
95
peo - - ple.
(non dim.)
F
a tempo
f
99
ff brillante
102
senza rall.
senza rall.
fff

# 8. O how amiable are thy dwellings

*(Duet for soprano and tenor)*

Psalm 84

A version of this movement for SATB choir with piano or organ is available in the USA from Hinshaw Music, Inc. (HMC-1393).

© Oxford University Press 1994, 1996

15
A
più ardente
mp
My soul hath a de-sire and long - ing
hosts!
più ardente
mp
My soul hath a de-sire and
mp
19
mp
to
long - ing to en - ter in - to the courts of the Lord:
22
cresc.
mf
en - ter in - to the courts of the Lord: my heart and my flesh, my
mf
my
cresc.

25
cresc.
f
heart and my flesh re - joice, re - joice in the liv - ing
cresc.
f
heart and my flesh re - joice, re - joice in the liv - ing
mf cresc.
f
28
God.
God.
un pochissimo meno mosso
B
p semplice
Yea, the spar-row hath found her an house,
un pochissimo meno mosso
B
dim.
p
32
Tempo I
p semplice
mp cresc.
and the swal-low a nest where she may lay her young: e-ven thy al - tars, O Lord of
Tempo I
cresc.
mp

37
mf
e-ven thy al - tars, O Lord of hosts, my King and my
hosts, e-ven thy al - tars, O Lord of hosts,— my King and my
f
41
God, my King and my God.
C
mp
Bless - ed are
dim.
45 (SOPRANO SOLO)
they—— that dwell in thy house: they will be al - - - - way
48
prais - ing thee, al - - - - way prais - ing thee.

TENOR SOLO
mp
cresc.
mf
Bless-ed is the man whose strength is in thee: in whose heart are thy ways, in whose heart are thy ways.
dim.
p
Ped.
D
pp
O Lord God of hosts, hear my prayer:
p dolce
hearken, O God of Jacob, hearken, O God of Jacob.
mf
risoluto
Be-

67
mf risoluto
Be-hold, O God our de - fend - er: and look up-on the face of thine An -
-hold, O God our de - fend - er: and look up-on the face of thine An -
mf
E
Poco più mosso ( ♩ = c. 66 )
70
p
mp elato ma tranquillo sempre
-oint - ed. For one day in thy courts: is bet-ter than a
-oint - ed.
dim.
p
sim.
Ped.
74
thou-sand.
mp dolce sempre
I had ra-ther be a door-keep-er in the house of my God:
mp

79
mp
For the
mf
than to dwell in the tents of un - god - li - ness.
mf
mp
F
83
mf
cresc.
f
mf
Lord God is a light and de - fence, the Lord God is a light and de - fence: the
the Lord God is a light and de - fence:
trem.
poco a poco rallentando
89
Lord will give grace and wor - ship,
the Lord will give grace and
dim.

G Tempo I ( ♩. = c. 56 )
92
mp
and no good thing shall he with -
wor - ship, and no good thing shall he with -
G Tempo I ( ♩. = c. 56 )
95
cresc.
- hold from them that live a god - - - - - - - ly
mf dolce
- hold from them that live a god - - - - - - - ly
99
p
life.
life.

102
mp dolce
H
mf
O Lord God of hosts: bless - ed is the
mp dolce
mf
O Lord God of hosts: bless - ed is the
H
mp
mf
105
mp
poco rit. al fine
p
man that put - teth his trust in
mp
p
man that put - teth his trust in
poco rit. al fine
mp
108
thee.
thee.
p

# 9. O praise the Lord of heaven

*(for double choir SATB–SATB)*

Psalm 148

Also available separately from Hinshaw Music Inc. (HML-505). Some minor changes have been made in this edition, which is not fully compatible with the separate publication.

© Hinshaw Music Inc. 1981, 1996

13
S.
A.
CHOIR 1
O praise the Lord of heav'n:
T.
B.
S.
A.
CHOIR 2
O praise the Lord of heav'n:
T.
B.
B
16
praise him in the height.
Praise him, all ye an - gels of his:
praise him in the height.
Praise him, all ye an - gels of

18
praise him, all his host.
Praise him,_ sun and moon:
his:
praise him, all his host.
Praise him,___ sun and moon:
Ped.
21
praise him,_ all ye stars_ and light.
C
unis.
Praise him,_ all ye hea-vens,_
praise_ him, all ye stars and light.
C

24
cresc.
praise him, all ye hea - vens: and ye wa - ters that are a -
cresc.
unis. f
cresc.
Praise him, all ye hea-vens, praise him, all ye hea - vens: and ye wa - ters that are a -
unis.
f
cresc.
cresc.
27
ff
f sonore
unis.
-bove the heav'ns. Let them praise the Name of the Lord: for he
unis.
ff
f sonore
ff
unis. f sonore
-bove the heav'ns. Let them praise the Name of the
unis.
ff
f sonore
ff
f

30
spake the word, and they were made, they were made; he com-
Lord: for he spake the word, and they were made;
33
-mand-ed, and they were cre - a - ted.
he com-mand-ed, and they were cre - a - ted.

D
36
f marcato
He hath made them fast for ev - er and ev - er:
f marcato
f marcato
He hath made them fast for ev - er and
f marcato
D
38
cresc.
allarg.
ff
he hath giv-en them a law which shall not be bro - ken, which shall not be
cresc.
ff
cresc.
ff
ev - er: he hath giv-en them a law which shall not be bro - ken, which shall not be
cresc.
ff
allarg.
cresc.
ff

41
E
Vivace ( ♩ = 144 )
bro - ken.
bro - ken.
sfp
ff
f
Ped.
48
F
( ♪ = ♪ )
p cresc.
ALTOS
CHOIRS
1 and 2
unis.
Praise the Lord up-on earth,
praise the
TENORS
p ritmico
cresc.
mf
dim.
p

mp cresc.
mf
Lord up - on earth, praise the Lord up - on earth: ye
mp cresc.
mf
mp
cresc.
mf
unis.
(Choirs 1 and 2 divide)
dra - gons, and all deeps;
dim.
mp
G
mp
mf
f
Ch. 1 Praise the Lord, praise the Lord, praise the Lord up - on
mp
mf
f
mp cresc.
mf cresc.
f
Ch. 2 Praise the Lord, praise the Lord, praise the Lord up - on
mp cresc.
mf cresc.
f
G
mf
f

75
f
earth. Fire and hail, snow and va - pours: wind and storm, ful - fill - ing his
f
earth.
Ped.
Ped.
83
word;
f
Fire and hail, snow and va - pours: wind and storm, ful - fill - ing his word;
f
mp

92
H
mp
mf
Praise the Lord,
praise the Lord,
praise the Lord,
p
mp
mf
p cresc.
mp cresc.
mf cresc.
Praise the Lord,
praise the Lord,
praise the Lord,
p cresc.
mp cresc.
mf cresc.
H
p
cresc.
mp
cresc.
mf
cresc.
98
f
ff
praise the Lord,
praise the Lord up - on earth,
f
ff
f cresc.
ff
praise the Lord,
praise the Lord up - on
f cresc.
ff
f
cresc.
ff

104
ff
(Choirs 1 and 2 unis.)
praise the Lord up - on earth.
ff
(Choirs 1 and 2 unis.)
earth, praise the Lord up - on earth.
mp
p
I
SOPRANOS
(Choirs 1 and 2)
111
p dolce
(♩ = ♩)
Moun - tains and all hills: fruit - ful trees and all ce - dars;
TENORS
(Choirs 1 and 2)
Moun - tains and all hills: fruit - ful trees and all ce - dars;
p dolce
I
(♩ = ♩)
legato

118
ALTOS
(Choirs 1 and 2)
p dolce
J
worms and fea - ther'd fowls;
Beasts and all cat - tle:
TENORS
(Choirs 1 and 2)
Praise the Lord,
BASSES
p dolce
(Choirs 1 and 2)
p ritmico
J
ritmico
mp
123
mf
f
praise the Lord,
praise the Lord up - on earth.
Kings of the earth and all peo - ple:
mp
mf
f
mf
f
131
più f
K
prin - ces and all ju - dges of the world;
più f
K

139
ff
f
148
ALTOS
(Choirs 1 and 2)
L
( ♪ = ♪ sempre )
mf leggiero
A.
Young men and mai - dens, old men and chil - dren,
mf
155
praise the Name of the Lord: for his Name on - ly is ex - cel - lent,
TENORS
(Choirs 1 and 2)
mf leggiero
T.
Young men and mai - dens, old men and chil - dren, praise the Name
162
M
and his praise a - bove hea - ven and earth. Praise the Name
of the Lord, the Name of the Lord: for his Name
BASSES
(Choirs 1 and 2)
mf leggiero
B.
Young men and mai - dens, old men and
M

168
SOPRANOS
(Choirs 1 and 2)
mf leggiero
S.
Young men and mai - dens,
A.
of the Lord, praise the Name of the Lord. Young men and mai - dens,
T.
on-ly is ex-cel-lent, praise the Lord.
B.
chil - dren, praise the Name of the Lord: for his
mp
mf
174
old men and chil - dren, praise the Name of the Lord, praise the Lord.
old men and chil - dren, praise the Name of the Lord, praise the Lord.
and his praise a-bove hea-ven and earth.
Name on-ly is ex-cel-lent, and his praise a - bove the earth.

181
N
(Choirs 1 and 2 divide)
Praise the Name of the Lord, the Name of the
Praise the Name of the Lord, the Name of the
Praise the Name of the Lord, the Name of the
Young men and maidens, old men and children, praise the Name of the
dim.
187
O
p legato
S.
A.
Lord.
Young men and maidens, old men and
T.
B.
p legato
p
mf dim.
mp
Lord, the Name of the
Lord:
and his praise above heaven and
Lord: for his Name only is excelent,
mp ritmico
mf
dim.
p

193
chil - - dren, praise the Name of the
all his saints shall praise
mp
earth.
He shall ex - alt the horn of his peo - ple;
for his
all his saints shall praise
mp
mp
for his
199
Lord.
P
(Choirs 1 and 2 unis.)
(p)
O praise the Lord of heav'n:
Lord.
him.
(Choirs 1 and 2 unis.)
p
Name only is ex - cel - lent.
O praise the Lord of heav'n:
him.
Name only is ex - cel - lent.
P
pp cresc.
p
Ped.
*

205
S.
A.
T.
B.
p
mf cresc.
praise him in the height.
Praise the Lord of
mf
Praise the Lord of heav'n,
mp
praise him in the height.
Praise the Lord of
praise the Lord of heav'n,
praise the Lord of heav'n,
cresc.
mp
mf
Ped.
sim.
214
f cresc.
ff
Q
heav'n,
praise the Lord of heav'n, O
praise the Lord of heav'n:
praise the Lord of heav'n,
O
praise the Lord of heav'n:
heav'n,
praise the Lord of heav'n, O
praise the Lord of heav'n:
praise the Lord of heav'n,
O
praise the Lord of heav'n:
f
cresc.
ff
marcato

223
praise him in the height. Praise him, all ye an - gels of his: praise him,
praise him in the height. Praise him, all ye an - gels of his: praise him,
praise him in the height. Praise him, all ye an - gels of his: praise him,
praise him in the height. Praise him, all ye an - gels of his: praise him,
mf
f
232
R
Poco più mosso ( ♩ = 156 )
mf
all his host. Praise him, sun and moon;
all his host. Praise him, sun and moon;
all his host. Praise him, sun and moon;
all his host. Praise him, sun and moon;
R
Poco più mosso ( ♩ = 156 )
mf
f

238
(Choirs 1 and 2 divide)
praise him, sun and moon:
praise him, sun and moon:
dim.
mf
f
dim.
243
f cresc.
S
ff
S.
A.
praise him, all ye hea - vens, praise him,
T.
B.
f cresc.
ff
mf cresc.
f cresc.
ff
praise him, all ye hea - vens, praise him, all ye hea - vens, praise
mf cresc.
f cresc.
ff
S
mf cresc.
f cresc.
ff

248
allargando
cresc.
praise him, praise him, praise him. A - - - - - - - -
cresc.
cresc.
him, praise the Lord, praise the Lord of
cresc.
allargando
254
fff
Meno mosso ( ♩ = 96 )
-men. A - men.
fff
fff
heav'n. A - men.
fff
Meno mosso ( ♩ = 96 )
fff
sffp
ff
fff
f
sffz

# TEXTS

### 1. O be joyful in the Lord

O be joyful in the Lord, all ye lands: serve the Lord with gladness, and come before his presence with a song. Be ye sure that the Lord he is God: it is he that hath made us, and not we ourselves; we are his people, and the sheep of his pasture. O go your way into his gates with thanksgiving, and into his courts with praise: be thankful unto him, and speak good of his Name. For the Lord is gracious, his mercy is everlasting: and his truth endureth from generation to generation. O be joyful in the Lord, all ye lands. Glory be to the Father; glory be to the Son: and to the Holy Ghost; as it was in the beginning, is now, and ever shall be: world without end. Amen.

*(Psalm 100)*

### 2. I will lift up mine eyes

I will lift up mine eyes unto the hills: from whence cometh my help. My help cometh even from the Lord: who hath made heaven and earth. He will not suffer thy foot to be moved: and he that keepeth thee will not sleep. Behold, he that keepeth Israel: shall neither slumber nor sleep. The Lord himself is thy keeper: the Lord is thy defence upon thy right hand; So that the sun shall not burn thee by day: neither the moon by night. The Lord shall preserve thee from all evil: yea, it is even he that shall keep thy soul. The Lord shall preserve thy going out, and thy coming in: from this time forth for evermore. Amen.

*(Psalm 121)*

### 3. Praise the Lord, O my soul

Praise the Lord, O my soul; while I live will I praise the Lord: yea, as long as I have any being, I will sing praises unto my God. O put not your trust in princes, nor in any child of man: for there is no help in them. For when the breath of man goeth forth he shall turn again to his earth: and then all his thoughts perish. Blessed is he that hath the God of Jacob for his help: and whose hope is in the Lord his God; Who made heaven and earth, the sea, and all that therein is: who keepeth his promise for ever; Who helpeth them to right that suffer wrong: who feedeth the hungry. The Lord looseth men out of prison: the Lord giveth sight to the blind. The Lord helpeth them that are fallen: the Lord careth for the righteous. The Lord careth for the strangers; he defendeth the fatherless and widow: as for the way of the ungodly, he turneth it upside down. The Lord thy God, O Sion, shall be King for evermore: and throughout all generations. Glory be to the Father, and to the Son, and to the Holy Ghost; As it was in the beginning, is now, and ever shall be: world without end. Amen.

*(Psalm 146)*

### 4. The Lord is my shepherd

The Lord is my shepherd: therefore can I lack nothing. He shall feed me in a green pasture: and lead me forth beside the waters of comfort. He shall convert my soul: and bring me forth in the paths of righteousness, for his Name's sake. Yea, though I walk through the valley of the shadow of death, I will fear no evil: for thou art with me; thy rod and thy staff comfort me. Thou shalt prepare a table for me against them that trouble me: thou hast anointed my head with oil, and my cup shall be full. But thy loving-kindness and mercy shall follow me all the days of my life: and I will dwell in the house of the Lord for ever.

*(Psalm 23)*

### 5. Cantate Domino

*Cantate Domino canticum novum.* O sing unto the Lord a new song: sing unto the Lord, all the whole earth. Sing unto the Lord, and praise his Name: be telling of his salvation from day to day. Declare his honour unto the heathen: and his wonders unto all people. For the Lord is great, and cannot worthily be praised: he is more to be feared than all gods. As for all the gods of the heathen, they are but idols: but it is the Lord that made the heavens. Glory and worship are before him: power and honour are in his sanctuary. Ascribe unto the Lord the honour due unto his Name: bring presents, and come into his courts. O worship the Lord in the beauty of holiness: let the whole earth stand in awe of him. Let the heavens rejoice, and let the earth be glad: for he cometh to judge the earth.

*(from Psalm 96)*

| | |
|---|---|
| Veni Creator Spiritus, | *(Come Creator Spirit,* |
| Mentes tuorum visita: | *Visit the minds of your people:* |
| Imple superna gratia | *Fill with your divine grace* |
| Quae tu creasti pectora. | *Their hearts.)* |

*(9th-century hymn)*

*Cantate Domino canticum novum.*

### 6. The Lord is my light and my salvation

The Lord is my light and my salvation; whom then shall I fear: the Lord is the strength of my life; of whom then shall I be afraid? Though an host of men were laid against me, yet shall not my heart be afraid: and though there rose up war against me, yet will I put my trust in him. One thing have I desired of the Lord, which I will require: even that I may dwell in the house of the Lord all the days of my life, to behold the fair beauty of the Lord, and to visit his temple. For in the time of trouble he shall hide me in his tabernacle: yea, in the secret place of his dwelling shall he hide me, and set me up upon a rock of stone. Therefore will I offer in his dwelling an oblation with great gladness: I will sing, and speak praises unto the Lord. Hearken unto my voice, O Lord, when I cry unto thee: have mercy upon me, and hear me. My heart hath talked of thee, Seek ye my face: Thy face, Lord, will I seek. O hide not thou thy face from me: nor cast thy servant away in displeasure. Thou hast been my succour: leave me not, neither forsake me, O God of my salvation. When my father and my mother forsake me: the Lord taketh me up. Be strong, and he shall comfort thine heart; and put thou thy trust in the Lord.

*(from Psalm 27)*

**7. O clap your hands**

O clap your hands together, all ye people: O sing unto God with the voice of melody. For the Lord is high, and to be feared: he is the great King upon all the earth. He shall subdue the people under us: and the nations under our feet. He shall choose out an heritage for us: even the worship of Jacob, whom he loved. God is gone up with a merry noise: and the Lord with the sound of the trump. O sing praises, sing praises unto our God: O sing praises, sing praises unto our King. For God is the King of all the earth: sing ye praises with understanding. O clap your hands together, all ye people.

*(from Psalm 47)*

**8. O how amiable are thy dwellings**

O how amiable are thy dwellings: thou Lord of hosts! My soul hath a desire and longing to enter into the courts of the Lord: my heart and my flesh rejoice in the living God. Yea, the sparrow hath found her an house, and the swallow a nest where she may lay her young: even thy altars, O Lord of hosts, my King and my God. Blessed are they that dwell in thy house: they will be alway praising thee. Blessed is the man whose strength is in thee: in whose heart are thy ways. O Lord God of hosts, hear my prayer: hearken, O God of Jacob. Behold, O God our defender: and look upon the face of thine Anointed. For one day in thy courts: is better than a thousand. I had rather be a door-keeper in the house of my God: than to dwell in the tents of ungodliness. For the Lord God is a light and defence: the Lord will give grace and worship, and no good thing shall he withhold from them that live a godly life. O Lord God of hosts: blessed is the man that putteth his trust in thee.

*(from Psalm 84)*

**9. O praise the Lord of heaven**

O praise the Lord of heaven: praise him in the height. Praise him, all ye angels of his: praise him, all his host. Praise him, sun and moon: praise him, all ye stars and light. Praise him, all ye heavens: and ye waters that are above the heavens. Let them praise the Name of the Lord: for he spake the word, and they were made; he commanded, and they were created. He hath made them fast for ever and ever: he hath given them a law which shall not be broken. Praise the Lord upon earth: ye dragons, and all deeps; Fire and hail, snow and vapours: wind and storm, fulfilling his word; Mountains and all hills: fruitful trees and all cedars: Beasts, and all cattle: worms, and feathered fowls; Kings of the earth and all people: princes and all judges of the world; Young men and maidens, old men and children, praise the Name of the Lord: for his Name only is excellent, and his praise above heaven and earth. He shall exalt the horn of his people; all his saints shall praise him. O praise the Lord of heaven: praise him in the height. Praise him, all ye angels of his: praise him, all his host. Praise him, sun and moon: praise him, all ye heavens, praise him, praise the Lord of heaven. Amen.

*(Psalm 148)*